ANARCHIVAL PRACTICES

Worlding Public Cultures

This publication series investigates the global dimensions of contemporary public culture through the concept of 'worlding', an understanding of the world generated through continuous processes of world-making. The deployment of 'worlding' in this series builds on the postcolonial project of critiquing universalized Eurocentric frameworks, and is committed to a radical ontology of relationality. Going beyond current top-down models of inclusion, diversity, and other representations of the global, the series critiques radical alterity in favour of a pluriversality attendant to entanglements, difficult histories, and power relations. It grounds the global within local and transculturally/transnationally intertwined worlds, and foregrounds the possibility of continuously making and re-making new worlds through the arts.

ANARCHIVAL PRACTICES
The Clanwilliam Arts Project as Re-imagining Custodianship of the Past

CARINE ZAAYMAN

ici
BERLIN PRESS

ISBN (Print): 978-3-96558-043-5
ISBN (PDF): 978-3-96558-044-2

Worlding Public Cultures
ISSN (Print): 2939-9211
ISSN (Online): 2939-922X

Bibliographical Information of the German National Library
The German National Library lists this publication in the Deutsche
Nationalbibliografie (German National Bibliography); detailed
bibliographic information is available online at http://dnb.d-nb.de.

In Europe, the print edition is printed by Lightning Source UK Ltd., Milton
Keynes, UK. See the final page for further details.

The digital edition can be downloaded freely at:
https://doi.org/10.37050/wpc-ca-01.

ICI Berlin Press is an imprint of
ICI gemeinnütziges Institut für Cultural Inquiry Berlin GmbH
Christinenstr. 18/19, Haus 8
D-10119 Berlin
publishing@ici-berlin.org
press.ici-berlin.org

Contents

Note on Parallel Text

During 2021 I conducted the fieldwork for this text, which included interviews with various members of the Clanwilliam Arts Project. I am deeply grateful for having been able to listen to their reflections and wanted to give space to some of their insights. However, I did not want to simply co-opt their words into my own argument, nor relegate them to appendices. Thus, I chose to include excerpts from these interviews alongside my writing (pages 30, 32, 34, and 36), especially since they testify powerfully to the transformative moments experienced during the project in ways to which my words cannot do justice.

Note on Images in the Text

Most images in this book are photographs that I took during a field trip to Clanwilliam in 2021. They are a record of my presence in the landscape and the town itself, as well as the site at the edge of the settlement where the Clanwilliam Arts Project staged its performances. I consider myself primarily a visual researcher, with my thinking spatial and relational in the first instance. The process of taking photographs and working through them afterwards was a core part of my reflection on the situatedness of the Clanwilliam Arts Project, the ideas that the landscape elicits, and insights that may be intuited by being there. Omitting these photographs would amount to leaving out a core component of my argument. I have thus elected to interweave them with my text, uncaptioned. Moreover, since my text troubles any notion that the past can be 'archived', I have resisted relying solely on documentary material from the project or pressing images into service as 'illustrations'. Nevertheless, it would be a disservice to the readers were they not able to get a sense of the spectacular nature of the parades and performances. Consequently, I include (captioned) photographs by Mark Wessels taken at various instantiations of the Clanwilliam Arts Project on pages 24, 25, 30, and 31.

FACING THE PAST

> The dilemma then, is how to
> grasp, narrate and transcend
> the unfinished business of
> colonialism and apartheid
> and to lay to rest all sorts of
> ghosts that continue to haunt
> post-apartheid South Africa.[1]

Where is the past? We carry personal memories in our minds and bodies, but we also carry stories of occurrences at which we were not present — even from times that precede our births—that we know through what others have told us.[2] In European colloquy (among others) there exists a tendency to imagine the past as being 'behind' us as we look 'forward' to the future. And yet we continuously narrate the stories that we carry mentally and bodily, thereby inserting them in the present. One can thus argue that the past is not really behind us, but *with* us, constantly imagined and re-imagined in public discourse through historical narrations. However, the creating of these historical narratives necessarily provokes a question of sources: what kind of material is apposite to serve as the foundation for the stories we tell of the past, stories that need to account for the wounds we (particularly those of us living in places deeply disrupted by European colonialism) are suffering in the present, but that should also help chart the futures we want? In this chapbook, I engage this challenge of sources.

I reflect critically on the habitual use of archives in the production of knowledge, and submit that other, extra-archival modes of historical narration are vital to the work of restorative justice and restitutive knowledge. Such work is a mode of maintaining custodianship of the past distinct from the historical preservation with which archive is conventionally credited.

I offer an example of extra-archival historical narration via my exploration of the Clanwilliam Arts Project. This long-term and collaborative undertaking, led annually by Magnet Theatre in the town of Clanwilliam, South Africa, employed artistic methodologies to produce a multivalent performance staged by school learners from the region.[3] While their project drew on stories from a colonial archive, Magnet did not use this archive to script the performances. Instead, the project instantiated a parallel life between the archive and the stories told to the learners by their parents.[4] The Clanwilliam Arts Project brings to light two vital concerns attending historical narrations in post-apartheid South Africa. The first is the pressing need to grapple with the legacies of colonialism and apartheid that still shape the institutions dominating the production of these narratives, such as archives, universities, and museums. The second is the capacity of various artistic methodologies to engage the extra-archival ways in which people find meaningful connection with a past that has, through the operations of colonialism and apartheid, been relegated and hidden.

In this chapbook, I want to respond to the challenge of finding ways to access and make visible relegated pasts by

proposing the 'anarchive',[5] a term that reconfigures archives in terms of absence rather than presence. It denotes the vast set of things characterizing the experience of being-in-the-present that cannot, by definition, be archived, but yet lives intangibly on into the present. Using the concept of the anarchive, I argue that the Clanwilliam Arts Project has employed what I term an 'anarchival practice', a mode of artistic production that, being deeply cognizant of the limits of colonial archives, focuses on giving voice to knowledges of the past that are embedded in a community.

My argument is articulated from a position deeply rooted in a particular place, namely South Africa. Even

after more than two decades since the formal abolition of apartheid, South Africa is still in the throes of negotiating — in a faltering way — its reverberations. The legacies of apartheid vibrate within almost every fibre of South African life. Struggles with this legacy find significant expression in activism and artistic production that seek both to tell different stories and to tell stories differently. These artistic and activist endeavours abound with feeling, and yet are born from pressing material needs. The abundance and urgency of such work compels me (among countless other South Africans) to better understand its stakes, strategies, and yields.

ARCHIVES: FRUSTRATIONS AND FUTILITY

Legislative apartheid might be particular to the history of
South Africa, but it was enabled by successive colonial oc-
cupations by European powers that shattered the worlds of
Khoekhoe and |xam[6] people who lived in Southern Africa
before the arrival of the settlers.[7] These colonists wreaked
devastation by forcibly controlling the lives of Khoekhoe
and |xam people (as well as various others entangled in the
colonial network). The devastation they caused extended to
both the material world and the symbolic realm. Through
colonization, Europeans enforced their hierarchies of race,
notions of value, and not least, ways of knowing
onto the parts of the world they occupied.
These symbolic and systemic structures
persist into the present within the institutions of government, civil so-
ciety, and education. The intangible or epistemic afterlives of
colonialism mean that even
after the end of colonialism
and apartheid, the infra-
structures that today
need to perform the
task of redress are
still governed by
colonial modes of
reasoning and or-
ganization.

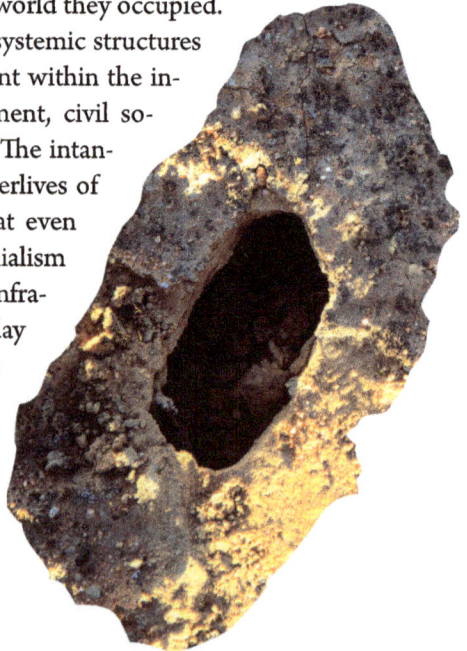

Ann Laura Stoler terms the persistence of these intangible colonial frameworks in the present 'duress'. She employs this term to indicate that it is active, a force at work — one that leaves its traces on the incorporeal aspects of life: 'Duress [...] has temporal, spatial, and affective coordinates. Its impress may be intangible, but it is not a faint scent of the past. It may be an indelible if invisible gash. It may sometimes be a trace but more often an enduring fissure, a durable mark.'[8]

Stoler notably argues that duress and colonial durability are exercised through colonial archives that continue to play a central role in the production of knowledge in the contemporary moment. She questions the aptness of employing colonial archives in the unfinished task of reckoning with colonial afterlives:

> The analytical tools we use to identify either historical continuities or, alternatively, profound ruptures from the past may be obstacles rather than openings. Colonial archives can impede the task: they have a way of drawing our attention to their own scripted temporal and spatial designations of what is 'colonial' and what is no longer, making it difficult to stretch beyond their guarded frames. Qualified and celebrated memories black out censored ones.[9]

That colonial archives can hinder rather than enable access to the past is an observation that people who are in the process of forging post-apartheid worlds, like those in Clanwilliam, already understand.

Despite the apparent problems with colonial archives
in a post-colonial world, it is nevertheless difficult to unset-
tle their status as pre-eminent sources, due to the formaliza-
tion of knowledge production in the discipline of History.
As Jason Lustig demonstrates, archives were positioned as
foundational evidence in the process of legitimizing History
as a scientific discipline in the nineteenth century.[10] Lustig
holds that even if archives were understood to be indirect
and incomplete records of the past, they were nevertheless
employed, even privileged, as sources uniquely able to pro-

vide access to the past: 'It constitutes an unspoken assump-
tion underpinning claims to knowledge of the past — that
sources, especially but not exclusively those held in archives, present a means to encounter semi-reliably a past that
otherwise would remain inaccessible — and even of the
present.'[11] Lustig argues that due to the way archives were
positioned in the nineteenth century, they are still granted
special epistemic status, even if their fidelity to the past has
always been understood to be partial and indirect.

Perhaps the most significant challenge to the purposiveness of archives has been directed not at what they hold,
but at what they omit, especially in reference to colonial
archives where official records were produced by colonial

powers and in their service. As Michel-Rolph Trouillot cogently observes,

> Silences enter the process of historical production at four crucial moments: the moment of fact creation (the making of sources); the moment of fact assembly (the making of archives); the moment of fact retrieval (the making of narratives); and the moment of retrospective significance (the making of history in the final instance).[12]

Trouillot signals here that silences pervade every stage of the production of historical narration. Such pervasiveness means that archives cannot be mobilized without actively acknowledging these silences. As Verne Harris contends, if archives are seen to be the repositories of memory, their slightness presents a problem: 'So archives offer researchers a sliver of a sliver of a sliver. If, as many archivists are wont to argue, the repositories of archives are the world's central memory institutions, then we are in deep amnesic trouble.'[13]

Even when acknowledged, the inherent limitations of archives pose a formidable challenge to knowledge production. Archival silences become especially vexing when colonial archives are employed in attempts to recoup 'lost' or 'omitted' stories, that is, in the fleshing out of stories that

were only very incompletely recorded.[14] Partial visibility in
the archives has meant that pressure is continuously exerted
on the few people who are included, and these small slivers
of life represented in the archives are made to stand in for
everyone and everything that has been left out. The intense
pressure exerted on these slivers of archival information on
such figures to tell stories far beyond than what they contain should therefore come as no surprise. In South Africa
(among other post-colonies), the absence of representation of most of the population (colonized people who are
now in the process of re-making their countries) from the
archives constitutes a present crisis: the absence is in the
first instance evidence of the oppressive effects of colonialism, while in the second instance it precludes people from
establishing a history of their own outside of the colonial
narrative. In the face of absence caused by colonial oppres-
sion, the post-colony embarks on a series of endeavours to
populate the archive *post facto*. As these activities are driven
by a desire to articulate and manifest identity separate from
(or in rebellion against) colonial structures, material that
exceeds conventional archival holdings is sought.

Due to their widely acknowledged bias and sparseness,
colonial archives are insufficient as custodians of the past,
and in many instances can even be understood to prevent
a meaningful connection to it. Being denied custodianship
of your own past can and has been experienced as a trauma,
which Margaret Iversen defines as 'an experience that has
failed to achieve a representation, but on which, nonethe-
less, one's whole existence depends'.[15] It is in this vein that

the absences in the archive can be understood as traumatic — they do not, and cannot find representation, but nevertheless shape the lives we live.

What then, are we to do with this loss, these absences? We cannot conjure away the silences even if we, as we must, approach colonial archives suspiciously. Such silences only intensify the desire for (impossible) representation and produces a melancholy in its frustration. This melancholy becomes especially pronounced in times and spaces where there is a need, as it were, to resurrect the dead. The presence of ancestors is called for, but the voices of ancestors are irreversibly excluded from the 'official' archives. There is no robust archive, at least in the conventional conception of archive as repository of documents, to counter the colonial ones. Counter-colonial identity can therefore not be founded on an appeal to archives alone. If colonial archives are of limited use on our path of repair and redress, then we should instead be guided to seek other modes in which the past is 'held'. Paradoxically, it is the silences that offer a place from which to begin looking for such other modes.

FACING THE SILENCE: THE ANARCHIVE

Seeking to loosen the ossifying grip archival material has habitually held on historical narration, I wanted to find discursive and methodological means to reveal the extent of absence in archives, particularly those fashioned along the lines of colonial epistemology and in its service. The conse-

quence of the centralization of absence is that archives are shown to be proportionately trivial, and if perceived in this relationship of scale, their capacity to control what can be known and narrated about the past is rendered absurd.

My frustration with the incapacity of colonial archives to answer the needs of a postcolonial and post-apartheid so-

ciety led me to focus on the troublesome archival silences themselves and grapple with their implications. To this end, I conceived the anarchive as a sign denoting everything that is absent from archives — understood in a profoundly expanded sense.[16] The anarchive refers to everything that cannot, by definition, be contained in archival documents, including the full sensorial experience of lived life — its non-linear temporality, unrealized potentials, and immaterial networks of intersubjectivity. Whereas archives as a medium can be said to filter out much of the intangible experience of lived life, the anarchive is contrariwise defined by them. Being founded in the intangible, the anarchive brings into view the vastness of absence in archives, since such absences refer not merely to that which *might* have been recorded but incidentally was not, or that which *was* recorded but subsequently lost. Rather, the anarchive is constituted by that which in the first place escapes the documentary matrices that make archives possible. What is more, the anarchive locates custodianship of the past not in archives, but in various other, intangible forms. Consequently, an anarchival methodology to making history (whether in formal or informal ways, in written, spoken or performative modes) eschews exclusive reliance on slivers of archival material as evidence.

Even though it reframes the relationship between archive and evidence, the anarchive does not suggest archives have no value; rather, it locates their value in the imprints of absence that archives hold, the ways in which they can help bring into view what is *not* there. From an anarchival standpoint, archives are invaluable not so much for preserving strands of the past, but rather for making visible the imprints of the absences of that which they fail to contain. I contend that this is the future productivity of archives: to enable us to see the imprints of absences within them.

Moreover, even though all archives are haunted by the anarchive, certain colonial archives, often those that are vast and rich in detail, are particularly well-placed to hold imprints of the presences that are absent from them, and are consequently more generative of work that makes the anarchive perceptible, sensible. Whereas Historiography, as developed and exported from Europe, has instrumentalized archives as constituting the limits of what is considered evidence, the anarchive makes us aware that there are many other sources we might draw on as we narrate the past. Thus, the   anarchive offers a constellation

of 'archive'   in which the   written,   colonial   docu-ment can no longer act as   the despot of historical narration, especially where it concerns the histories of people relegated by colonialism. Instead, the anarchive privileges other practices whereby we perform our custodianship of the past, practices that keep alive memories and ways of knowing in defiance of coloniality.

As I will show, performances such as those produced in the Clanwilliam Arts Project seize on some of the intangible, anarchival modes of historical narration, constituting the past not at a distance from the present, cut off from it, but as intangibly present around us, kept alive by other means than archival document. The power of anarchival practices such as these lies precisely in the embodied, incommensurable instantiation of experience and memory that allows for remaking the very worlds displaced by colonialism, even if only partially, imperfectly, and by necessity re-imagined for the present.

The anarchive invites forms of critical and creative engagement with colonial archives which disrupt scholarly protocols that accord colonial archives the power to delimit methodological possibilities when the past is engaged. However, while the anarchive configures archives in terms of absences, anarchival practices are not bent on filling these absences by means of reconstruction. Rather, the anarchive invites other methodological tactics, which I understand on three levels: first, as concerns scholarly and/or artistic engagement with colonial archives for the

purposes of 'fact retrieval', the anarchive insists that absence should be overtly acknowledged and held firmly in view. Absence in archives may be intimated by looking for its imprints, that is, a reading methodology driven by the desire to see absence. Second, with the compilation, or indeed the deeming,[17] of archives, the anarchive invites a reimagining of what archival formation, authorship, and ownership might mean. It welcomes the inclusion of both materials and systems of organization that eschew colonial categories, for example oral, affective, sensorial, intangible, and invented material, produced through processes that are co-designed and born from dissensus.[18] Lastly, the implication of the anarchive for historical narration is that forms of representation/narration other than those constrained by archive can productively articulate decolonial realities and subjectivities.

Since the anarchive relies on imagination and inventiveness, it is particularly suited to function as a basis for the work of artists who labour to address legacies of the past. The anarchive invites us to reimagine the forms of historical narration that emerge when conventional definitions of historical narration are jettisoned. Consequently, in the making of history, the anarchive embraces the inclusion of extra-archival materials and the yields of oral, affective, sensorial, inventive, embodied methodologies. The Clanwilliam Arts Project is an example of such a methodology, in that it puts a colonial archive to work unconventionally, by not staging its contents, but rather by employing it as a prompt to give form to the anarchive.

CLANWILLIAM: LANDSCAPE OF PAST AND PRESENT

Clanwilliam lies around 230 km north of Cape Town, South Africa. A small town in the mountainous Cederberg region, it is nestled in a landscape famed for its rock art sites, where it is thought more such sites are yet to be discovered.[19] The Cederberg area has one of the densest collections of rock art in the world, with instances ranging from as far back as eight thousand to between a hundred and two hundred years ago.[20] Due to the richness of archaeological deposits in the area, the landscape of the Cederberg has been the focus of much scholarly attention. Moreover, over the last three decades, the lower Cederberg area has seen significant developments in rock art tourism alongside a bourgeoning Rooibos tea industry.[21] Despite these developments in tourism and agriculture, Clanwilliam town remains economically depressed relative to the City of Cape Town. It is marked by a disparity between the opulence of its archaeological, cultural, and botanical heritage, and the economic realities faced daily by its inhabitants.

Contributing to this disparity, at least in part, is a tendency within institutional scholarship to overlook Khoekhoe and |xam perspectives in the production of knowledge on rock art as well as their own histories. Such neglect is one of the persistent legacies of colonialism embodied in the institutions of South Africa, in that the forms of 'knowing' practised by descendants of the Khoekhoe and |xam are consistently dismissed as inferior to Western forms such as the disciplines of archaeology, anthropology, and art history. Recent efforts to decolonize scholarship at South African universities have consequently centred on questioning the epistemological frameworks inherited from Europe, and instantiating forms of knowing that have existed — unrecognized — in other forms by 'first nations' people.[22]

June Bam's 2021 book, *Ausi Told Me*, is exemplary of such criticism. Bam argues that 'the everyday, decolonial-knowledge ecologies of the Cape Flats provide important pointers for reimagining the hybridised, precolonial pasts'.[23] She goes on to state that her book seeks to challenge the conventional assumption by 'the predominantly male, Eurocentric, liberal, African neocolonial "extinction" discourse that San and Khoi people at the Cape virtually all died out, along with their knowledge and cultural practices, in the smallpox epidemics of the 1700s'.[24] As Bam argues, the extinction narrative concerning Khoekhoe and |xam people takes no account of the ways in which their descendants in so-called coloured communities all over the Western and Northern Cape retained practices and knowledges from their forebears. In this way, the extinction narrative allowed

institutional scholars to both dominate the production of knowledge on Khoekhoe and |xam pasts and presents and shape the discourse around the perspective of Western institutional disciplines. Clanwilliam, as a site from which knowledge is produced, is emblematic of the way in which colonialism is perpetuated in the present through the oper-

ations of institutional scholarship. Dislodging such colonial
dominance necessitates first a critical evaluation of how colonial archives have legitimated certain kinds of knowledge,
and second, defamiliarization of naturalized structures of
what constitutes 'history'.

The work of Diana Taylor offers one avenue towards
such critique and defamiliarization. Taylor argues that the
logic of archive contributes to a colonial shaping of historical narration:

> Colonial history — with its logic of linear-
> ity — privileges unique, remarkable events.
> It entails a cultural value judgment, and
> strives for a definitive account of people and
> places, although everyone accepts that it is
> always being revised. Through documents
> and documentation, this kind of history has
> not only foregrounded its own story, with its
> own protagonists, it has also dispossessed
> those who could not prove their claims to
> lands, discoveries, or protagonism through
> deeds and titles.[25]

Taylor advocates a different approach to making history, one that recognizes other forms of
historical record, like those conveyed through
generations in embodied practices: 'Performances such as
the one I describe tell a different history — one that is all
about people and place, but not in any linear sense.'[26] The
configuration of historical narration suggested by Taylor
produces no timeline of events and no clear past or present.
Historical narration, in her work, does not need to focus on

singular events or individual people, but can instead relate the ways in which people in the present and the past share a commonality, though not replication, of experiences and ways of being. Since a space like Clanwilliam, especially in the post-apartheid moment, is marked by economic disparity and a dispossession of heritage, finding and amplifying continuities with a past relegated by institutional history-writing is a key part of doing counter-colonial work. The Clanwilliam Arts Project is one such undertaking.

PERFORMANCE AND PARADE

The Clanwilliam Arts Project was a long running, multi-disciplinary event initiated by LLAREC (the Lucy Lloyd Archive Resource and Exhibition Centre), and later coordinated by Magnet Theatre, a drama company based in Cape Town.[27] It was held in Clanwilliam for a week in September every year from 1998 to 2018.[28] Comprising various educational workshops, the event culminated in a parade through the town in which a |xam story, sourced from the Bleek and Lloyd archive, was dramatized. The Bleek and Lloyd collection, primarily compiled by German philologist Wilhelm Bleek and his sister-in-law Lucy Lloyd, is an important collection that includes |xam stories, drawings and watercolours, and constitutes the largest repository of information on |xam life in documentary format.[29] It is possibly one of the most utilized archives in South Africa, and has thus been subjected to a vast array of interpretative methodologies. Many scholars have laboured intensely to identify its colonial entanglement, and sought to find ways to see beyond the colonial frame. It is not an archive that has been treated as intransigent by any means.[30]

Magnet Theatre organized the project for the bulk of its duration, employing facilitators from the Drama, Music, and Fine Art departments of the University of Cape Town, as well as ComNet and other independent practitioners working in community arts training.[31] The facilitators presented workshops to around seven hundred school learners from Clanwilliam in art, drama, dance, lantern making, storytelling, drumming, stilt walking, and fire performance. One facilitator described the production of materials in the workshops as follows:

> The props that we made for the parade, the procession, were either small triangular lanterns for the children to carry, or massive animal sculptures that needed five or six of us to push along. The children built the small lanterns and a few of us made the larger animals. We used reed sticks for the structures and covered them in paper that we coated with wheat paste. Then we added candles to create the light sculptures that would accompany the children to the showgrounds on the night of the procession. We cut stacks of animal faces from cardboard for the children to paint and glitter, and feathers to make masks for them to wear. There was also the drama component where some children acted out the narrative, and the dance component where they could express themselves with body movements. There was a band where the older kids could play the sound effects for the story, and

Figures 1 and 2. Moments from two Clanwilliam Arts Project parades and per-formances, 2014 and 2010. Photographs by Mark Wessels.

Figure 3. A large light sculpture made for a Clanwilliam Arts Project event, 2014. Photograph by Mark Wessels.

a shadow puppet segment of the play. So it was a
wide range of expressive modes through which
this one written story could be sort of fleshed out
in a very visually and experientially interesting
way for not just the children, but the larger community as well.[32]

As the culmination of each year's workshop, the learners
and facilitators staged a lantern parade and a performance
of that year's story from the Bleek and Lloyd archive to an
audience of between two thousand five hundred and three
thousand people from the town.[33] Each year, a story that
might make sense to a contemporary audience and allow
for interpretation and performance was chosen from the
Bleek and Lloyd collection by Pippa Skotnes.[34] Magnet
then introduced the story to the workshop participants, and
engaged with it using 'a variety of artistic modalities *in order
to find the importance or significance of the story for their lives.
For ten years the same set of stories, the same methodology,
the same broad outcome: a parade through the streets with
lanterns and a performance of the story for the community.*'[35]

The Clanwilliam Arts Project drew on the connections to the Clanwilliam community and schools established by the Living Landscape Project, an initiative that sought to create employment opportunities for people living in landscapes where rock art was created.[36] Samuel Ravengai explains that 'one of the major aims of the Living Landscape Project was to empower these youths by giving them knowledge that would enrich the school curriculum and create opportunities for small business, such as rock-art guides'.[37] I understand this initiative to be in response, and possibly out of resistance, to extractive scholarly practices that neglect to reciprocate source communities for knowledge gained in locales where research was conducted.

Skotnes, an artist and scholar who has been engaging |xam and !kun histories for decades, was instrumental in developing the Clanwilliam Arts Project with the initial aim to 'introduce Bleek and Lloyd stories to a community who had been taught over several hundred years to reject anything to do with "Bushmen" and present them in a way that was meaningful to the learners and, critically, beautiful'.[38] She

invited Mark Fleishman to collaborate on the project early on. Skotnes and Fleishman emphasize that framing the Clanwilliam Arts Project as an artistic one is deeply rooted in |xam cosmology, intended to do justice to the nature of how (his)stories are communicated in these societies:

> Oral societies perform, rather than tell stories. In all San societies, storytelling and performing is a central part of social interaction and a way of creating both a shared art form and a shared history. For stories in such a tradition, to be written down and never performed again, is a kind of death. The story is trapped within the pages of a book, its life as an invisible presence on the wind, curtailed.[39]

Ravengai notes that in '2001 the project took on a visual and performance art dimension through the incorporation of Mark Fleishman and his Magnet Theatre into the performing of the archive and re-archiving that memory back into the Clanwilliam landscape'.[40] Similar to the Living Landscape Project, Magnet Theatre declares its intention

to invest resources into the area, rather than to extract knowledge, and do so by returning |xam 'heritage' to the descendant community of Clanwilliam: 'The Clanwilliam Arts Project includes archaeology, education, art and drama and is *aimed at returning the heritage of the Clan-william area to the community.*'[41]

Lavona de Bruyn, a long-time participant in and researcher of the Clanwilliam Arts Project, articulates how the material dispossession of descendants of the |xam and enslaved people effected by colonialism still marks the area of Clanwilliam, and emphasizes how this plays into the heritage industry in the area:

> Coloured identity in Clanwilliam is rooted in tensions between |xam, the English settlers and *trekboers* [...].[42] The different racial groups in the town still live in the separate areas demarcated by the Group Areas Act of 1950, even though this act was repealed in 1991. A process of interior de-colonization has affected ethnic minorities who possessed reserves of memory but little or no historical capital. In Clanwilliam, for example, archaeological sites record the tangible history and cultural heritage of the |xam in the form of rock paintings; however the impact of colonization and apartheid caused the collapse of historical memory and the loss of the sense of the significance of these paintings for the coloured community.[43]

It is thus vital to understand the Clanwilliam Arts Project as an undertaking that responds to the separation of the tangible records of the |xam — the archives held in institutions across the Western Cape — and the loss or lack of such 'tangible' sources in the community itself, and even the relegation of the

There is this other mode of reality that is described, where a person can be as much an animal and a star and the equivalence of being is in question, compared to what our cognition would say. Obviously, the archive itself is — how much less than one percent of the oral

tradition is it? We don't know, but it's definitely way less than one percent because the oral tradition was like a library of knowledge, just so massive and so endless and it was all contained in the minds of the people.

~

Figure 4. A moment in the performance for the 2010 Clanwilliam Arts Project. Photograph by Mark Wessels.

Figure 5. A large light sculpture made for a Clanwilliam Arts Project event, 2013. Photograph by Mark Wessels.

She did tell me a lot of stories straight out of Bleek and Lloyd, I nearly fell over listening to some of them. She has moved from farm to farm to farm as an itinerant worker her entire life.

~

But one thing that I acknowledge is that it was powerful for good, because a whole world was constructed in those performances.

~

I think I definitely feel partial to the Bleek and Lloyd archive now, because this project opened it up for me in a way that no other archive was before. If you think about delving into an archive, or sifting through objects in

a dusty museum, those are physical experiences that allow for intriguing connections with historically rich objects and images. But, obviously, the Clanwilliam Arts Project is something entirely different. It is engaging with an archive in a way that brings it to life, that gives it vitality. You're teaching it to children, through painting, through acting, through dancing and singing and music and building things. When the drums beat in time with the she-rhinoceros's heavy footsteps, the kids can feel her presence reverberate in their chests. You're engaging with the archive in a range of mediums wider than I have ever experienced in my entire life, just in terms of the number of different mediums through which you explore the story. You could also say it's a very childlike experi-

ence, because you're presenting the story to children in a way that is accessible to them, and in a way that inspires them. What's more, the kids are also teaching you about their struggles and their interests and how the ideas in the narrative connect with their lives. There's an incredible amount of emotional and physical investment in a project like this.

~

There is a lot of cultural work and cultural meaning created out of this central narrative that is — I don't want to say new, because it's adapted from this point of inspiration. However, at the same time, the entire ten-day project (and the weeks leading up to it) was an incredibly generative and collaborative space that only existed because of this sin-

gular starting point, this singular narrative on which we overlaid our own sounds and images and movements. It is an interesting way of making the archive come alive. You live and breathe this tiny portion of the archive for twelve to fourteen hours a day, over ten intense days. And then it's gone. After the procession we would burn most of the stuff we made during the project. I don't believe the intention was ever to insert data into the archive, there was never an intention to fill any gaps that may have been present in the archive or enrich the archive. The intention was to bring a small piece of the archive to the children and the community in a very big, impactful way.

~

stories of the past held in the oral traditions of the community (as an aftereffect of the erasures of colonization and apartheid). However, the methodology adopted by Magnet was not one of 'educating' the workshop participants about their inheritance. Instead, the methods applied by Fleishman and his team largely involved using the stories from the Bleek and Lloyd archives as 'prompts' for the participants to make a connection with the set of stories. Skotnes, a major authority on the Bleek and Lloyd archive, quipped that the stories from the archive still exist in the community, but were not 'marked' in a special way as |xam knowledge, rather simply stories that 'the old people tell'.[44]

The approach employed by Magnet for the Clanwilliam Arts Project was aligned to their practice across their body of work, developed by Mark Fleishman and his team over a period of more than thirty years. Magnet's process is founded on the principles of 'Performance as Research', that is, using a source text to develop a performance through a collaborative workshop process. In the Clanwilliam Arts Project, Magnet used the Bleek and Lloyd Archive as a starting point for their non-deterministic method. Fleishman argues that the Performance as Research methodology is 'not a progressivist building towards a finality, nor a mechanistic unfolding of a predetermined plan in search of something it knows exists before the search begins'.[45] The resulting dramaturgical practice thus departs from the notion of 'script', positioning its engagement with the source text as a 'process that is more about dwelling than building'.[46]

What I do think started to happen, there is no doubt when we started to tell stories and bring the stories from the archive, into the project very consciously each year that there were elders in the community who said, 'oh we know that story, we've heard that version of the story'.

~

I suddenly thought this is an oddness that this stuff sits in the library, kind of hidden away from the world […] The Clanwilliam Project was an attempt to say, 'ok what would it actually mean to free these stories from the archive, what would it actually mean to bring these stories out of the UCT library and make them circulate within a community that geographically was on the margins of the territory that the |Xam occupied?'

~

If Magnet positions the archive not as a source of historical evidence that functions as a blueprint from which to build artistic representation, nor to stage a reproduction, this positioning is not simply a stylistic choice. It is a considered response to the epistemological challenges within archive itself, its inherent limits and silences. The Clanwilliam Arts Project might have culminated each year in a parade and performance, but this was not the main goal of the workshop. Instead, the making of things together, the telling of stories together and the making music and dancing together created moments that brought deep, collective memory to the surface, rewriting it for and in the present, and practising to keep it alive. As Fleishman related to me in an interview:

> In Clanwilliam we did not say, 'Here's a story from the Bleek and Lloyd Archive. We are going to teach you the story and now that we've taught you the story, we are going to teach you how to convert that story into a performance for an audience.' That would have been one approach, but we weren't doing that. Instead, we said, 'Here's a story. Let's throw it into the space and see what comes of it.' Then, using various modalities, whether making art with your hands, or singing songs, or dancing, or holding story-telling workshops and so on, we would explore that story. In these activities, the story itself was constantly bringing up thoughts for them. We also did not say, 'Here's a San story. You are a descendant of the San, therefore you must know the story.' It was much more along the lines of, 'Here's a story. Now let's play. And now that you're playing, things start to emerge. What are *you* seeing in

the story? What are *you* feeling? What is it bring-
ing up for *you*?' While the facilitators were busy
painting with the learners, or cutting out pictures,
making collages and so on, conversations happened. Through those conversations, things began
to emerge. The facilitators would then bring those
things back into our discussions. When we were
putting together the final performance, we would
use what emerged in those conversations as our inspiration. We were learning from *their* experiences
of the story. If someone then went on to claim that
the story you brought in is 'my story because I am
a descendant of the San', that is a secondary thing,
which wasn't really what we were trying to do in
the first instance.[47]

It is thus imperative not to instrumentalize how collective
memory surfaced during the long life of the project. I am
not suggesting that embedded, though relegated, memories
(in the form of the stories) were lying like gold nuggets in
a riverbed, waiting to be recovered in one go. The Clanwilliam Arts Project did not set out to capture latent memor-
ies of |xam stories within the community of Clanwilliam.
Moreover, Magnet had no preconceived idea of how the
performance(s) would manifest, only which methodologies they wanted to use in response to the concomitance of
Clanwilliam as a site and the Bleek and Lloyd archive. Over
the long period that the Clanwilliam Arts Project operated,
Magnet and the project facilitators worked collaboratively
with young people from the area to listen to faint echoes
and surface strands, and to make more graspable the scat-
tered, indistinct, and dynamic embedded histories.

Through years of iterations, the project found its form and thus the effects of the work accumulated. Fleishman suggested in the same interview:

> What I think art practices do, is that they produce the conditions from which, if you pay attention and learn to run alongside, rather than fixating on capturing what emerges through the process of practicing a particular art form, then knowledge will be there. The extent to which you can pay attention to it will allow you to say something about that knowledge or to learn from it.[48]

The way in which Magnet Theatre developed this methodology consciously drew on Diana Taylor's conception of the 'repertoire' — an intangible form of shared memory and the performance of a set of practices and routines, where there is (often unarticulated) significance embedded in this repertoire for those who perform it. In *The Archive and the Repertoire, Performing Cultural Memory in the Americas* (2003), Taylor advocates identifying repertoires as sources of knowledge that are distinct from archive: 'We learn and transmit knowledge through embodied action, through cultural agency, and by making choices. Performance, for me, functions as an episteme, a way of knowing, not simply an object of analysis.'[49] Taylor thus posits the notion of a deep repertoire, shared by members of a community, that functions to maintain and convey knowledge, including knowledge of the past. Hence, repertoire is a form of embodied 'archive', but an archive that does not exist in textual form or inside institutional buildings. What is more, repertoire relies on recurring performance and is not 'petrified' at the point of entering the archive. Its preservation depends on repeated performances, themselves introducing incremental shifts, additions, and omissions.

By drawing on extra-archival ways of knowing, Taylor's 'repertoire' is aligned with the anarchive and the reframing of what it means to have custodianship of the past.[50] We should nevertheless not think of the repertoire as being an 'alternative' to conventional archive, but rather as a term that recognizes the everyday, and mostly unmarked ways in which people practise being custodians of the past and produce pertinent historical narration for and about themselves. While repertoire is not an alternative to archive, it does help us to hold the limitations of archive in view, to see clearly that so-called concrete archival evidence is no substitute for memory. The anarchive and practices that embody it make apparent how contingent the memories that shape our lives are on the intangible, the affective, and the communal. Consequently, performances such as those produced by the Clanwilliam Arts Project seize on some of the anarchival forms in which the past is present around us, in this instance as 'old stories', the telling of which instantiates a repertoire. What is more, instantiating this repertoire does not serve simply to 'resurrect' a past, but to offer an opportunity for beginning anew, for self-fashioning identities from sources rendered taboo by colonial forms of knowing.

SIGNAL TO ANARCHIVAL NOISE

The Clanwilliam Arts Project is characterized by an interpretative promiscuity that generates a complicated
end-product, itself not easily digested by established institutional frameworks. Ravengai, for example, claims that the
Clanwilliam Arts Project's performances are too loosely
connected to the Bleek and Lloyd archive.[51] For him, these
new texts, brought into being through the workshops prior
to the parade, are haunted too faintly by the ghost of the
'original story'. While noting that because of its freer interpretation of the archive, the new text 'infiltrates the theo-
logical [original] text and dispossesses it of its authorial
power',[52] Ravengai nevertheless criticizes the new text as being mostly 'noise'. And noise, he contends, will not 'engender
collective action to solve the problem'.[53] I am troubled that
his argument hinges on the Clanwilliam Arts Project's lack
of fidelity to the archival material. Since colonial epistemes
shaped the very existence of Bleek and Lloyd, I would argue
that any engagement with the archive needs to account in a
robust manner for this entanglement, not treat it as an inert
source in which //Kabbo's world has been (fragmentally)
preserved.[54] In fact, in a postcolonial and post-apartheid
present, archives such as the Bleek and Lloyd collection can
be said to *demand* the kind of engagement that expands the
type of stories that can emerge from it, as well as who might
be authoring those stories.

The project's creatively chaotic engagement with the
Bleek and Lloyd archive resonates with the work of vari-

ous scholars, writers, and artists who have attempted to deal with the complexity of colonial entanglement, what colonial archives are silent on, and what they are *not* able to tell us about the past. In her influential essay, 'Venus in Two Acts', Saidiya Hartman, for example, proposes a methodology of 'critical fabulation' as a possible way to engage critically with an archive in which the subjugated (enslaved people in the case of her essay) have no voice, while refusing to be constrained to the limits of that archive.[55] As concerns the archives of slavery, Hartman argues,

> History pledges to be faithful to the limits of fact, evidence, and archive, even as those dead certainties are produced by terror. I wanted to write a romance that exceeded the fictions of history — the rumors, scandals, lies, invented evidence, fabricated confessions, volatile facts, impossible metaphors, chance events, and fantasies that constitute the archive and determine what can be said about the past. I longed to write a new story, one unfettered by the constraints of the legal documents and exceeding the restatement and transpositions, which comprised my strategy for disordering and transgressing the protocols of the archive and the authority of its statements and which enabled me to augment and intensify its fictions.[56]

By referring to the 'fictions of history', Hartman reminds us that archives are themselves not mere records of fact, but formed in part by attempts to quell unknowns, uncertainties, and anxieties.[57] In response to the friable, fragmentary nature of archives, as well as the hosts of absences that haunt them, Hartman asks whether it is 'possible to exceed or negotiate the constitutive limits of the archive'.[58] In order to do so, she proposes to engage in a methodology of 'critical fabulation':

> By advancing a series of speculative arguments exploiting the capacities of the subjunctive (a grammatical mood that expresses doubts, wishes, and possibilities), in fashioning a narrative, which is based upon archival research, and by that I mean a critical reading of the archive that mimes the figurative dimensions of history, I intended both to tell an impossible story and to amplify the impossibility of its telling.[59]

For Hartman, critical fabulation is not intended to recover the lives of those left out of archives, but rather to enact *at the same time* the possibility of what those lives *could* have been as well as the *impossibility* of truly knowing what they were. Moreover, Hartman advocates critical fabulation as a method with an eye on the present, to 'imagine a free state, not as the time before captivity or slavery, but rather as the anticipated future of this writing'.[60]

Note Hartman's invocation of 'noise' as a powerful signifier of resisting the narrative embedded in the archive:

Narrative restraint, the refusal to fill in the gaps and provide closure, is a requirement of this method, as is the imperative to respect black noise — the shrieks, the moans, the nonsense, and the opacity, which are always in excess of legibility and of the law and which hint at and embody aspirations that are wildly utopian, derelict to capitalism, and antithetical to its attendant discourse of Man.[61]

Whereas Ravengai criticizes the Clanwilliam Arts Project for producing noise, in Hartman's logic, noise can instead be understood as productive in that it gives shape to that which archives obscure. If framed in this way, noise signals the presence of something whose meaning is not indexed through the archive, or through colonial epistemes — it remains semantically locked.

In relation to the Clanwilliam Arts Project, the experience of 'noise' during the workshop, the parade and the performance was due to the spectacular aspect of the endeavour, which was also its power, immersing a large number of people in the excitement and thrust of the moment. As he outlines the conceptual frame of his body of work, Fleishman likewise emphasizes the significance of noise when enunciating outside of colonial vocabularies. For him, noise holds the power 'to disrupt the situation, to initiate events that have the capacity to transform the situation, the regime of established knowledge'.[62] This disruptive power comes from the capacity of noise to exist as an expression, but still remain closed to interpretation. Fleishman articulates this opacity of noise in relation to Daniel Defoe's novel *Robinson Crusoe*:

> The problem posed by the footprint in the sand (what Crusoe fears most) is not that it does not speak, it is that when its voice is finally heard (when Friday eventually shows himself), it manifests through one of two modalities: as a 'cry' — unintelligible, beyond recognized language and in need of treatment — or through the body as vehicle of language — either docile […] or wild, disordered, undisciplined, disruptive, violent. In other words, when allowed to speak it threatens the capacity of translation, of 'scholarly exegesis'.[63]

When considering Hartman's invocation of archival absence, it is crucial to note that she does not suggest that these absences can be imaginatively filled, or that the loss can be reconstructed. Rather, she posits that this absence *remains* unfathomable in the grids of intelligibility established in and through the archives. To speak to this absence, and to articulate what it produces, a different representational vocabulary is called for. If one interpolates the Clanwilliam Arts Project's performances with Hartman's critical fabulation, then their infidelity to the Bleek and Lloyd archive and their production of 'noise' can be understood both as giving

expression to the archive and as conjuring its anarchive. The performance/parade employs the archive as but one source of the past while also giving voice to embodied, intuitive, and unconscious extra-archival knowledge that already exists within the community in which it is staged — although never given due recognition.

  Anarchival practices do not resolve the paradoxes of inscrutability and the uncontainable nature of the anarchive. Such practices might render the anarchive sensible, but once sensible, the anarchive can still not be captured in the archive. Moreover, by remaining steadfastly outside the 'grids of intelligibility', anarchival practices themselves resist being archived, and are thus profoundly tied to the moments and spaces in which they occur. While performance as such is notoriously difficult to document, with the Clanwilliam Arts Project (understood as employing anarchival

practices) the question of what remains becomes especially difficult to name. At the conclusion of every year's performance, the props were burnt. While some photographs of the workshops, parades, and performances exist, they cannot fully convey the spectacle, the immersion or the *noise* of the events. Likewise, this text must reduce the fullness of the project to description and quotation.

The last iteration of the Clanwilliam Arts Project took place in 2018, and as it moves into the realm of the past, measuring its impact is tricky. Instead of looking for quantifiable effects, we need to develop a broader sense of the purposiveness of anarchival practices. We may begin by reading the effects of such practices in the vistas of the imagination they are able to open. Conducting the research for this chapbook left me with a strong sense of the indelible impression the project made on everyone involved. Over time the Clanwilliam Arts Project came to demonstrate to the participants and facilitators alike the power of the old stories and how they connect the people of Clanwilliam to a past denied to them for so long by colonialism and apartheid. We may yet find the yields of this resurrected connection in unexpected places.

MAKING HISTORY FROM THE ANARCHIVE

> Dark times, Hannah Arendt tells
> us, surround us when the past
> cannot guide us into the future.
> Our work towards decolonisa-
> tion is taking place in just such a
> dark time, both because it cannot
> be theorised in advance (there
> is very little received wisdom),
> and because we are now in an
> extremely unstable time of ever
> more rapid change.[64]

Macroscopic and granular views are at play in this text, as
is perhaps the nature of a case study. I began this chapbook
by indicating that I would focus on the specificities of the
South African context, but it is not exceptional in having to
confront the persistent legacies of colonialism. South Africa shares the burden of dealing with the institutional and
structural afterlives of colonialism with other post-colonies
and settler colonies across the globe. By explicating what
the interplay between archive and repertoire in the Clanwilliam Arts Project brought forth over the many years it
occurred, I hope to contribute a perspective from the South
that could aid in the broader project of liberating the making of history from colonial duress.

The Clanwilliam Arts Project offers an example of how artistic methodologies can creatively mobilize some of this colonial inheritance to lead us beyond colonial logics. I have argued that by reframing archive in terms of absence — by engaging the anarchive — we are able to access the intangible and inchoate ways in which the past remains with us. Moreover, the anarchive makes visible the embodied, affective modes in which people maintain and assert custodianship of the past, as well as the ways they give expression to the stories that for them resonate in the present. The anarchival methodology applied by Magnet Theatre in the Clanwilliam Arts Project, I have argued, provides an example of how colonially-shaped archives can be pressed into service not only for the purposes of evidence or reconstruction, but as a prompt to bring out latent or relegated knowledges of the past.

At the heart of an anarchival reframing of sources is the desire to recognize the shifting nature of how knowledge is generated, to accept that we are always operating from a position of *not-knowing*. It might be reasonable to look 'back' on the past from the position of knowing 'what happened next' but lived experience does not occur in the face of known futures. Rather than lamenting a lack of certainty, anarchival practices offer the possibility of keeping the past radically open, consciously and continuously finding and making connection and meaning from it. Due to this openness, we should not be surprised that the forms of expression generated through anarchival practices do not readily yield to interpretative methodologies that would fix meaning, especially those of institutional scholarship. Artistic practices, by contrast, with their developed modes of associative representation, are better suited to evoke through their forms the ambiguities and intangibilities with which conventional archival materiality struggles to contend. I suggest that the decolonial yield of anarchival practices lies in this re-forming of historical narration, of finding ways to counter the habitual positioning of colonialism as being 'past', engaging instead with how it persists and where it needs to be undone.[65]

NOTES

1   Bhekizizwe Peterson, 'Spectrality and Inter-generational Black Nar-
     ratives in South Africa', *Social Dynamics*, 43.3 (2019), pp. 345–64
     (p. 356).
2   Within the field of Memory Studies, such oral, intergenerational
     transmission of memory is referred to as 'postmemory', a term not-
     ably developed by Marianne Hirsch. See, for instance, Marianne
     Hirsch, *Family Frames: Photography, Narrative, and Postmemory*
     (Cambridge: Harvard University Press, 1997.) This chapbook does
     not engage directly with this term, but I acknowledge the profound
     influence it has had on the recognition of inter-generational mem-
     ory. I understand postmemory to constitute one of the ways in
     which the past lives with us and consider it one of a host of concepts
     that resonate with the anarchive, which I developed in response to
     the frustration I experienced when seeking information about my
     ancestor, Krotoa. My focus in this chapbook, however, is especially
     on articulating a creative methodology that consciously engages a
     colonial archive *otherwise* in order to stage those memories and ren-
     der them visible.
3   Magnet Theatre worked closely with the Michaelis School of Fine
     Art, where the project originated, as well as other creative and per-
     forming arts departments at the University of Cape Town and some
     independent facilitators.
4   Private correspondence with Pippa Skotnes, 14 August 2022.
5   The 'anarchive' as a conceptual framework was developed during the
     course of my PhD work and had frequent exposure in the Archive
     and Public Culture initiative at the University of Cape Town. In this
     community I received invaluable contributions from its chair (and
     one of my thesis supervisors), Carolyn Hamilton, as well as my
     other supervisor, Pippa Skotnes, and the cohort of my peers who
     were likewise thinking through the complexities of archival work in

the Southern African context. For their input and feedback, I remain
deeply grateful.

6   I refer here to the two very broadly defined groups of people who
are considered to be 'indigenous' to the Western Cape area where
colonial occupation in Southern Africa took root, namely Khoekhoe
and |xam (sometimes referred to as Khoi/Khoikhoi and San). Im-
portantly, other groups of people who identified themselves by differ-
ent names and spoke different languages, such as N|uu or ≠khomani
for example, lived further inland at this time, and it should be noted
that no collective term is without problems of generalization or eli-
sion. Descendants of various groups of Khoekhoe and |xam are today
claiming identity as 'First Nations', though these claims are also not
without contestation. It should further be borne in mind that colonial
expansion into the interior of the country during the eighteenth and
nineteenth centuries brought about its own regime of violence and
domination enacted upon other communities, including isiXhosa,
isiZulu, Sotho people, and so forth.

7   Continuing colonial occupation of the Southern tip of Africa is
generally said to have begun in 1652 with the arrival of Jan van Rie-
beek and his men in the service of the VOC. During the Napoleonic
wars in the late eighteenth and early nineteenth century, the British
were given custody of the Cape by the Dutch. The British formally
possessed the Cape in 1806. Expansion into the interior was led by
Dutch-descendant *trekboers* (migrant farmers) during the nineteenth
century. South Africa became a union under the British Crown in
1910, and an independent nation in 1961.

8   Ann Laura Stoler, *Duress* (Durham: Duke University Press, 2016),
p. 6.

9   Ibid., p. 5.

10 Jason Lustig, 'Epistemologies of the Archive: Toward a Critique of
Archival Reason', *Archival Science*, 20.1 (2020), pp. 65–89 (p. 65)
<https://doi.org/10.1007/s10502-019-09313-z>.

11 Ibid., p. 66.

12 Michel-Rolph Trouillot, *Silencing the Past: Power and the Production of
History* (Boston: Beacon, 1995), p. 26.

13 Verne Harris, 'The Archival Sliver: Power, Memory and Archives in
South Africa', *Archival Science*, 2 (2002), pp. 63–86 (p. 65).

14 Partial visibility in the colonial archives pertaining to the Cape is at
play in a powerful manner in the VOC records, where certain Khoe-

khoe people make their appearance, for example Autshumao, Krotoa, Oudasoa, and Doman.

15 Margaret Iversen, 'Readymade, Found Object, Photograph', *Art Journal*, 63.2 (2004), pp. 44–57 (p. 47).

16 See my PhD thesis, *Seeing What is Not There: Figuring the Anarchive* (unpublished doctoral thesis, University of Cape Town, 2019). I was influenced by its usage in Jacques Derrida's 'Archive Fever: A Freudian Impression', trans. by Eric Prenowitz, *Diacritics*, 25.2 (1995), pp. 9–63, where it was connected to the forgetting that accompanies the archive, and where it slips away (see pp. 51 and 57). Other scholars and artists arrived at the term 'anarchive' independently, and use it to denote something different. For other instances of the term being used to refer to scholarship and cultural expression engaged with archive with an interest in inter-disciplinary production, performance, and the intangible, see the Montreal-based research group Senselab (senselab.ca) and the WalkingLab project (walkinglab.org). Hal Foster also used the term to describe the inclination of artists to evoke archival practices in his article 'An Archival Impulse', *October*, 110 (2004), pp. 3–22.

17 Verne Harris describes 'deeming' in relation to archives as 'an act of deeming such a trace to be worthy of protection, preservation and the other interventions which we call archival' in his article 'Genres of the Trace: Memory, Archives and Trouble', in *Archives and Manuscripts*, 40.3 (2012), pp. 147–57 (p. 150). He notes that such usage of the term is indebted to Carolyn Hamilton, especially as articulated in *Refiguring the Archive*, ed. by Carolyn Hamilton, Verne Harris, Jane Taylor, Michele Pickover, Graeme Reid, and Razia Saleh (David Philip: Cape Town, 2001).

18 Cf. Ann Laura Stoler, 'On Archiving as Dissensus', *Comparative Studies of South Asia, Africa and the Middle East*, 38.1 (2018), pp. 43–56.

19 Cf. Janette Deacon, Nicholas Wiltshire, and Rika du Plessis, 'Designing Digital Recording for Volunteers in Rock Art Surveys, Management Plans and Public Outreach in the Cederberg, South Africa', *African Archaeological Review*, 35.2 (2018), pp. 225–39.

20 Cf. John Parkington, 'Clanwilliam Living Landscape Project', *Nordisk Museologi*, 1 (1999), pp. 147–54, and *Khoisan Rock Art* <https://www.cederberg.co.za/environment/khoisan-rock-art> [Accessed 27 February 2022].

21 Rooibos is a plant endemic to the Cederberg area, and is used in the

production of a tea that is characteristic of this location. For a fuller exploration, see Boris Gorelik, 'Rooibos: An Ethnographic Perspective: A Study of the Origins and Nature of the Traditional Knowledge Associated with the *Aspalathus linearis*', Rooibos Council (2017) <https://sarooibos.co.za/rooibos-an-ethnographic-perspective/> [Accessed 27 February 2022].

22 It should be noted that the term 'First Nations' is not accepted by everyone within the discourse on Khoekhoe and |xam histories and identities, largely because the term is sometimes seen as an import from the West, and considered an unhelpful generalization.

23 June Bam, *Ausi Told Me: Deep Listening and Intergenerational Knowledge from the Cape* (Auckland Park: Fanele, 2021), Kindle ebook.

24 Ibid.

25 Diana Taylor, 'Performance and/as History', *TDR*, 50.1 (2006), p. 83.

26 Ibid.

27 It should be noted that this chapbook does not aim to provide a thick ethnography of the Clanwilliam Arts Project. While, lamentably, none such exists, this text is focused on making visible the methodological yields of the project within the framework of decolonizing scholarship that grapples with a colonial archive.

28 These dates are based on the entirety of the project's duration, from before Magnet took over its organization.

29 The Digital Bleek and Lloyd website enumerates its collection as follows: 'The Digital Bleek and Lloyd includes scans of every page of the 110 Lucy Lloyd |xam notebooks, 17 Lloyd (mostly) !kun notebooks and 28 Wilhelm Bleek |xam notebooks. It also includes Jemima Bleek's solitary Korana and !kun notebook and four Lloyd Korana notebooks in the Maingard collection of the Library at the University of South Africa, as well as Dorothea Bleek's 32 notebooks. All the drawings and watercolours made by |han≠kass'o, Dia!kwain, Tamme, |uma, !nanni and Da are also in the digital collection. The digital archive includes a 280 000-word searchable index, cross-referenced and including notes and summaries for each of the stories listed.' <http://lloydbleekcollection.cs.uct.ac.za/> [Accessed 10 August 2022].

30 For further information on the Bleek and Lloyd (sometimes referred to as the Lloyd and Bleek) collection, see, Lloyd and Bleek Collection, *World Heritage Sites: Africa*, JSTOR <https://www.aluka.org/

heritage/collection/LBC>, as well as *The Digital Bleek and Lloyd*, University of Cape Town, <http://lloydbleekcollection.cs.uct.ac. za/> [Accessed 22 February 2022 and 10 August 2022].

31   For footage of the workshops, see the short film, *The Mediation and Facilitation of a 'Living' Landscape Within the Musical Arts Through the Clanwillian Arts Project: A Short Documentary* by Brandon H. Andrews, Rebekka Sandmeier, and Veronica Baxter, video recording (2021) <https://doi.org/10.25375/uct.19990424.v1> [Accessed 10 August 2022].

32   Andrew Juries, interviewed by Carine Zaayman about the Clanwilliam Arts Project, 14 September 2021.

33   Clanwilliam Arts Project, *Magnet Theatre*, <https://magnettheatre. co.za/project/clanwilliam-arts-project/> [Accessed 22 February 2022].

34   Private correspondence with Pippa Skotnes, 14 August 2022.

35   Mark Fleishman, 'The Difference of Performance as Research', *Theatre Research International*, 37.1 (2012), pp. 28–37 (pp. 31–32). Emphasis added <https://doi.org/10.1017/S0307883311000745>.

36   Living Landscape Project, *The African Rock Art Digital Archive*, <http://ringingrocks.wits.ac.za/locations/public_rock_art_sites/ western_cape/living_lanscape_project/> [Accessed 22 February 2022].

37   Samuel Ravengai, 'Performing the Archive and Re-archiving Memory: Magnet Theatre's Museum and Reminiscence Theatre', *South African Theatre Journal*, 28.3 (2015), pp. 209–21 (p. 212) <https:// doi.org/10.1080/10137548.2015.1046398>.

38   Private correspondence with Pippa Skotnes, 14 August 2022. Skotnes notes the importance of the beauty of the performance produced by the Clanwilliam Arts Project, saying 'This was the great success of Mark Fleishman's contribution — his performances and the parade itself were truly beautiful' (ibid.).

39   Pippa Skotnes and Mark Fleishman, *A Story is the Wind* (Cape Town: LLAREC, University of Cape Town, 2002), p. 16.

40   Ravengai, 'Performing the Archive and Re-archiving Memory', p. 212.

41   Clanwilliam Arts Project, *Magnet Theatre*, <https://magnettheatre. co.za/project/clanwilliam-arts-project/> [Accessed 22 February 2022]. Emphasis added.

42   Apartheid classification of the South African population included the

category 'coloured', which referred primarily to descendants of enslaved people and/or those intermingled with Khoi and San groups.
The term is highly contested in contemporary South Africa, where it
is claimed by some as a politicized identity while rejected by others
as an unproductive inheritance of apartheid 'divide and conquer'
strategies.

43 Lavona de Bruyn, 'Catalysing a Community: Magnet's Clanwilliam
     Community Intervention Project', in *Magnet Theatre. Three Decades
     of Making Space*, ed. by Megan Lewis and Anton Krueger (Pretoria:
     UNISA Press and Bristol & Chicago: Intellect, 2015), Chapter 18
     (p. 257).

44 Pippa Skotnes, interviewed by Carine Zaayman about the Clanwil-
     liam Arts Project, 30 August 2021.

45 Mark Fleishman, 'Making Space for Ideas: The Knowledge Work of
     Magnet Theatre', in *Magnet Theatre: Three Decades of Making Space*,
     ed. by Megan Lewis and Anton Krueger (Pretoria: UNISA Press and
     Bristol & Chicago: Intellect), Chapter 2 (p. 57).

46 Ibid.

47 Mark Fleishman, interviewed by Carine Zaayman about the Clanwil-
     liam Arts Project, 13 September 2021.

48 Ibid.

49 Diana Taylor, *The Archive and the Repertoire, Performing Cultural
     Memory in the Americas* (Durham, NC : Duke University Press,
     2003), p. xvi.

50 Precolonial 'archives'/pasts are not temporally limited, thus, they
     do not cease to exist at the 'point' of colonial contact. These pasts
     remain, to this day, engaged in a struggle with colonial domination,
     and become visible/sensible at various points. The Khoekhoe and
     |xam archives are particularly pertinent examples of how precolonial
     archives are not 'lost', as well as the epistemological challenges that
     accessing them present. The anarchive as an idea emerged precisely
     in response to these challenges as embodied by the Khoekhoe and
     |xam legacies.

51 Ravengai, 'Performing the Archive and Re-archiving Memory',
     p. 215.

52 Ibid., p. 217.

53 Ibid.

54 //Kabbo is one of the central |xam interlocutors for Bleek and Lloyd and features prominently in the collection, and is positioned centrally by Ravengai.

55 Saidiya Hartman, 'Venus in Two Acts', *Small Axe*, 26, 12.2 (2008), pp. 1–14.

56 Ibid. p. 9.

57 Ann Laura Stoler provides persuasive evidence of how colonial archives are replete with inventions, in *Along the Archival Grain: Epistemic Anxieties and Colonial Common Sense* (Princeton: Princeton University Press, 2009).

58 Hartman, 'Venus in Two Acts', p. 9.

59 Ibid.

60 Ibid., p. 4.

61 Ibid., p. 12.

62 Mark Fleishman, *Remembering in the Postcolony: Refiguring the Past with Theatre* (unpublished doctoral thesis, University of Cape Town, 2012), p. 20.

63 Ibid., p. 95.

64 Deborah Bird Rose, *Reports from a Wild Country: Ethics for Decolonisation* (Sydney: University of New South Wales Press, 2004), p. 1.

65 I am indebted to various readers for their generous feedback during the writing of this paper, and wish to thank Pippa Skotnes, Wayne Modest, Chiara de Cesari, Carmen Robertson, and Deborah Thomas, as well as members of the Archive and Public Culture initiative at the University of Cape Town. Additionally, I am grateful to the members of the Worlding Public Cultures project for giving me the opportunity and support to develop this work. For taking the time to reflect on their experiences of the Clanwilliam Arts Project, I want to thank each of those whom I interviewed. A special thank you to Mark Wessels for providing photographs of the Clanwilliam Arts Project and granting permission for their usage in this publication. To the ICI, and in particular Christoph Holzhey, my enduring thanks for their flexibility with my layout and its effects on the production of this chapbook. Finally, I wish to express my sincere gratitude to Mark Fleishman for our conversations on the intellectual foundations of his and Magnet's work.

REFERENCES

Andrews, Brandon H., Rebekka Sandmeier, and Veronica Baxter, *The Mediation and Facilitation of a 'Living' Landscape Within the Musical Arts Through the Clanwillian Arts Project: A Short Documentary*, video recording (2022) <https://doi.org/10.25375/uct.19990424.v1>

Bam, June, *Ausi Told Me: Deep Listening and Intergenerational Knowledge from the Cape* (Auckland Park: Fanele, 2021)

Clanwilliam Arts Project, *Magnet Theatre* <https://magnettheatre.co.za/project/clanwilliam-arts-project/> [Accessed 22 February 2022]

de Bruyn, Lavona, 'Catalysing a Community: Magnet's Clanwilliam Community Intervention Project', in *Magnet Theatre: Three Decades of Making Space*, ed. by Megan Lewis and Anton Krueger (Pretoria: UNISA Press and Bristol & Chicago: Intellect, 2015), pp. 253–64

Deacon, Janette, Nicholas Wiltshire, and Rika du Plessis, 'Designing Digital Recording for Volunteers in Rock Art Surveys, Management Plans and Public Outreach in the Cederberg, South Africa', *African Archaeological Review*, 35.2 (2018), pp. 225–39 <https://doi.org/10.1007/s10437-018-9293-3>

Derrida, Jacques, 'Archive Fever: A Freudian Impression', trans. by Eric Prenowitz, *Diacritics*, 25.2 (1995), pp. 9–63 <https://doi.org/10.2307/465144>

The Digital Bleek and Lloyd <http://lloydbleekcollection.cs.uct.ac.za/> [Accessed 10 August 2022]

Fleishman, Mark, 'The Difference of Performance as Research', *Theatre Research International*, 37.1 (2012), pp. 28–37 <https://doi.org/10.1017/S0307883311000745>

—— *Remembering in the Postcolony: Refiguring the Past with Theatre* (unpublished doctoral thesis, University of Cape Town, 2012)

—— 'Making Space for Ideas: The Knowledge Work of Magnet Theatre', in *Magnet Theatre: Three Decades of Making Space*, ed. by Megan Lewis and Anton Krueger (Pretoria: UNISA Press and Bristol & Chicago: Intellect, 2015),   pp. 53–75

Foster, Hal, 'An Archival Impulse', *October*, 110 (2004), pp. 3–22 <https://doi.org/10.1162/0162287042379847>

Gorelik, Boris, 'Rooibos: An Ethnographic Perspective; A Study of the Origins and Nature of the Traditional Knowledge Associated with the *Aspalathus Linearis*', Rooibos Council (2017) <https://sarooibos.co.za/rooibos-an-ethnographic-perspective> [Accessed 27 February 2022]

Hamilton, Carolyn, Verne Harris, Jane Taylor, Michele Pickover, Graeme Reid, and Razia Saleh, eds, *Refiguring the Archive* (David Philip: Cape Town, 2001) <https://doi.org/10.1007/978-94-010-0570-8>

Harris, Verne, 'The Archival Sliver: Power, Memory and Archives in South Africa', *Archival Science*, 2 (2002), pp. 63–86 <https://doi.org/10.1007/BF02435631>

—— 'Genres of the Trace: Memory, Archives and Trouble', *Archives and Manuscripts*, 40.3 (2012), pp. 147–57 <https://doi.org/10.1080/01576895.2012.735825>

Hartman, Saidiya, 'Venus in Two Acts', *Small Axe*, 26, 12.2 (2008), pp. 1–14 <https://doi.org/10.1215/-12-2-1>

Hirsch, Marianne, *Family Frames: Photography, Narrative, and Postmemory* (Cambridge, MA: Harvard University Press, 1997)

Iversen, Margaret, 'Readymade, Found Object, Photograph', *Art Journal*, 63.2 (2004), pp. 44–57 <https://doi.org/10.1080/00043249.2004.10791125>

Khoisan Rock Art, Cederberg Conservancy <https://www.cederberg.co.za/environment/khoisan-rock-art> [Accessed 27 February 2022]

Lloyd and Bleek Collection, *World Heritage Sites: Africa*, JSTOR <https://www.aluka.org/heritage/collection/LBC> [Accessed 6 April 2022]

Lustig, Jason, 'Epistemologies of the Archive: Toward a Critique of Archival Reason', *Archival Science*, 20.1 (2020), pp. 65–89 <https://doi.org/10.1007/s10502-019-09313-z>

Parkington, John, 'Clanwilliam Living Landscape Project', *Nordisk Museologi*, 1 (1999), pp. 147–54 <https://doi.org/10.5617/nm.3603>

Peterson, Bhekizizwe, 'Spectrality and Inter-generational Black Narratives in South Africa', *Social Dynamics*, 43.3 (2019), pp. 345–64 <https://doi.org/10.1080/02533952.2019.1690757>

Ravengai, Samuel, 'Performing the Archive and Re-archiving Memory: Magnet Theatre's Museum and Reminiscence Theatre', *South African Theatre Journal*, 28.3 (2015), pp. 209–21 <https://doi.org/10.1080/10137548.2015.1046398>

Rose, Deborah Bird, *Reports from a Wild Country: Ethics for Decolonisation* (Sydney: University of New South Wales Press, 2004)

Skotnes, Pippa, and Mark Fleishman, *A Story Is the Wind* (Cape Town: LLAREC, University of Cape Town, 2002)

Stoler, Ann Laura, *Along the Archival Grain: Epistemic Anxieties and Colonial Common Sense* (Princeton: Princeton University Press, 2009) <https://doi.org/10.1515/9781400835478>

—— *Duress* (Durham, NC: Duke University Press, 2016)

—— 'On Archiving as Dissensus', *Comparative Studies of South Asia, Africa and the Middle East*, 38.1 (2018), pp. 43–56 <https://doi.org/10.1215/1089201x-4389967>

Taylor, Diana, *The Archive and the Repertoire, Performing Cultural Memory in the Americas* (Durham, NC: Duke University Press, 2003) <https://doi.org/10.1215/9780822385318>

—— 'Performance and/as History', *TDR*, 50.1 (2006), pp. 67–86 <https://doi.org/10.1162/dram.2006.50.1.67>

Trouillot, Michel-Rolph, *Silencing the Past: Power and the Production of History* (Boston: Beacon, 1995)

Zaayman, Carine, *Seeing What Is Not There: Figuring the Anarchive* (unpublished doctoral thesis, University of Cape Town, 2019)

Worlding Public Cultures

Series Editor
   Ming Tiampo

Managing Editor
   Eva Bentcheva

Assistant Managing Editor
   Kelley Tialiou

Copy Editor
   Francesca Simkin

Editorial Board
   Eva Bentcheva
   May Chew
   Chiara de Cesari
   Birgit Hopfener
   Paul Goodwin
   Alice Ming Wai Jim
   Monica Juneja
   Franziska Koch
   Wayne Modest
   Miriam Oesterreich
   Edith-Anne Pageot
   Ming Tiampo
   Maribel Hildago Urbaneja
   Toshio Watanabe

The publication series takes as its starting point 'Worlding Public Cultures: The Arts and Social Innovation' (WPC), a collaborative research project and transnational platform conceived by the Transnational and Transcultural Arts and Culture Exchange (TrACE) network in 2018.

WPC is funded by the Trans-Atlantic Platform for the Social Sciences and Humanities (T-AP) through a collaboration between the following granting agencies:

Dutch Research Council (NWO), Netherlands
Economic and Social Research Council (ESRC), UK
Federal Ministry of Education and Research (BMBF)/DLR Project Management Agency, Germany
Fonds de recherche du Québec — Société et culture (FRQSC), Canada
Social Sciences and Humanities Research Council (SSHRC), Canada

The WPC publication series is produced through the generous funding of ICI Berlin Institute for Cultural Inquiry, BMBF, NWO, FRQSC, SSHRC, and the National Museum of World Cultures, Netherlands.

REGISTERS IN THE SERIES
Troubling Public Cultures: Case Studies
These single and collaboratively-authored Case Studies explore 'worlding' in different regional, temporal, thematic, institutional, and practice-related contexts.

Worlding Concepts
Worlding Concepts serves as a lexicon of key terminology discussed and developed throughout the WPC project.

Academies
These edited volumes present contributions and discussions from WPC academies and assemblies.

Companions for Thinking and Doing
Companions distil the theoretical insights of the WPC project to provide practice-based reflections, proposals, and questions.

List of published titles at: https://doi.org/10.25620/wpc-print.